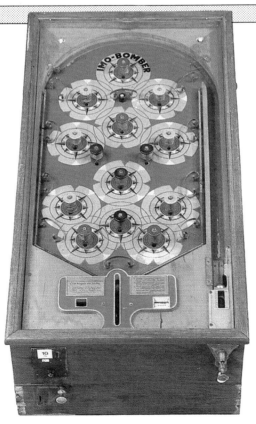

PINBALL

TIGER BOOKS INTERNATIONAL
LONDON

Picture credits:
Bally Wulff, Berlin (52); Deutsches Museum, Munich (2); Gauselmann group,
Espelkamp (31); Informationsgemeinschaft Münzspiel GmbH, Bonn (14);
Dieter Ladwig, Düsseldorf (1)

Translated by Phil Goddard
in association with First Edition Translations Limited, Cambridge
Text editor: Petra Raszkowski

CLB 3493
This edition published in 1994 by Tiger Books International PLC, London
by arrangement with CLB Publishing
© 1994 this English language edition CLB Publishing, Godalming, Surrey
Originally published in German by V.I.P.
© 1992 Paul Zsolnay Verlag Ges.m.b.H, Vienna
All rights reserved
Printed and bound in Italy
ISBN 1-85501-481-5

INTRODUCTION

A good pinball machine is like a Broadway musical, full of bright lights and high-speed movement. The noise of the thumper bumpers is like the tap dancing of *42nd Street* or *A Chorus Line*." So says Roger Sharpe, one of the leading experts on pinball machines and their history. It is an evocative, almost poetic description for a game which has been around for 60 years and still exerts a magnetic pull over devotees.

There are many reasons for the fascination of pinball machines. There is the unique combination of flashing lights and fast-moving action. There is the challenge of pitting your skill and tactical abilities against a machine, the high degree of concentration it requires and the excitement as your score mounts. There are no prizes at stake, and if you lose, all you have to do is insert another coin. That is where the pleasure lies.

Essentially, there are only three things you can do to affect which way the ball goes: the way you shoot it, the way you move the flippers, and tilting the machine. But each of these can make the difference between a high and a low score, a casual player and an expert. Whether you shoot the ball hard or gently depends on the layout of the machine. You will need to play the ball gently if you want to score more points on the top half of the playdeck, while if you want to hit the first targets particularly hard, you will need to play the ball accordingly.

Then there are the flippers, which are used to bring the ball back into play from the bottom or sides of the machine. These can be used to bring the ball to a halt and then fire it off in the direction where it is likely to score the most points.

Hardest of all is the technique of carefully tilting the machine to change the direction of the ball. "Carefully" is the operative word: if you overdo it, the machine will take umbrage, the word "tilt" will flash up and the game is over; sometimes you will also lose all your remaining plays. If you've ever seen a real expert doing this, you'll realize that the skill of the game does not just lie in careful manipulation of the flippers.

So pinball takes concentration, manual dexterity and physical control. But what kind of person is the typical player? In the Great Depression of 1930s America, there were huge numbers of unemployed men without the slightest chance of paid employment. Sitting in a bar, making a beer last a whole afternoon and playing this new game were a great way of whiling away the time at no great expense.

The 1950s were the age of rock and roll. The trademarks of this new generation, personified by James Dean, were leather jackets, jeans and T-shirts; another was their passion for pinball.

Since the 1970s, pinball machines have broadened their appeal, attracting people from all backgrounds and being played widely in bars, amusement arcades and even homes. But there is one thing which has not changed: people who play pinball tend to be rock music fans. The two have been particularly strongly associated since the cult movie *Tommy* (1974), with the Who's lead singer Roger Daltrey in the title role. Rock music and pinball are inextricably linked: you might almost say that the pinball machine was the star of the movie. It is from *Tommy* that the phrase "pinball wizard" comes.

There is one thing you can say about the typical player: he is male. There are far more male than female pinball fans, perhaps because the bright colors and vivid images of the playdeck and display mirror the ambitions of young males.

But this is the only constant feature of machine design: pinball machines have evolved continuously over the decades, reflecting changes in technology and in people's lifestyles. The purely mechanical machines of the early years gave way to the electric pintables of the "Golden Age" in the '50s and '60s. And even strong competition from video games in the computer era has failed to dent the popularity of pinball machines, which are more sophisticated and attractive than ever before. Like all their predecessors, they are a form of escape, inviting us to forget our everyday problems for a while and pit our skills against a machine. As one newspaper said in 1981:

"Pinball machines have an erotic, exotic appeal: they create remote dream worlds peopled by the likes of Tarzan, Superman and Batman, a dazzling profusion of images. The player is held in thrall by the steadily mounting score: any pinball fan will tell you that what happens on the pintables is not just a leisure activity: it's a way of life."

Once upon a time... Bagatelle and Pinball

C harles Dickens' novel *The Pickwick Papers,* written in 1836, describes a club which meets in a tavern to play bagatelle. It was this game, dating from the early 19th century, which formed the basis of our modern-day pinball. More specifically, it is a direct descendant of a game devised in the United States by Montague Redgrave in 1871, known as Improvements in Bagatelles.

The first coin-operated bagatelle game, the "Log Cabin," was introduced by the Sicking Manufacturing Company in 1880. Both of these early games already had three of the key features of the modern pinball machine:

1. The table was slightly tilted so that the ball rolled back toward the player.
2. Pins were placed around the holes to trap the ball.
3. The ball was brought into play using a spring mechanism.

Around the turn of the century bagatelle was an exceptionally popular game, but then it lapsed back into obscurity. The real turning-point occurred in 1929, when an American advertising representative, John J. Sloan, chanced upon an old bagatelle game. He liked the idea so much that he decided to turn it into a business, and began mass-producing the games and selling them for $100 each. This price was obviously far too high, and Sloan's business inevitably failed. But it had attracted the attention of a number of companies and inventors to the potential of this traditional game.

Abraham Lincoln, the 16th president of the United States, playing bagatelle

Much of the development of the pinball machine occurred in Chicago, which became the pinball capital of the world. Harry Williams, the Gottlieb brothers, Raymond T. Maloney and the Bingo Novelty Company are names which have gone down in pinball history; some are still in existence. They used Sloan's idea to develop bagatelle-based, coin-operated machines which were much closer to the machines we know today.

In 1931, Sol Gottlieb built the "Baffle Ball." This gave seven balls for a penny, which were played into pockets of various point values. At the same time Bingo brought out a machine called the "Bingo," and Maloney introduced the "Ballyhoo," named after a popular magazine. It was this machine that really marked the beginning of the pinball era. In only seven months, the company sold around 50,000 machines at $16 apiece.

Maloney founded the Bally Manufacturing Company, which became the market leader. The earliest machines were table-mounted, with no legs, though floor machines were produced soon afterwards.

Against all expectations, pinball machines immediately became hugely popular in Europe. American manufacturers seem to have forgotten that the idea of bagatelle had been well known in Britain for decades. Montagne, a US manufacturer and owner of British American Novelty, told his British partner Adickes skeptically: "You may have learned a little about amusement machines, but these amusing bagatelle tables will never catch on in London."

He was wrong. The first two European pinball machines were manufactured by Keeney, and known as the "Rainbow" and "Diamond Table." These were being used in the White Horse Inn in London in late 1931.

Sales of pinball machines expanded very rapidly despite, or perhaps because of, the Depression. Further improvements were made, and the original glass marbles were replaced with today's steel balls. In 1933, a machine was developed with flaps which closed when the ball fell into the hole; the first hit opened the way to another hole with a higher score.

The tilt mechanism was introduced as early as 1934, to prevent the machine from being tilted to change the path of the ball; this form of cheating was already widespread. Machines were also weighted down with sandbags, and sharp needles were placed on the undersides to stop them being lifted. The tilt mechanism, which ended the game if the player cheated, was clearly visible in the early machines, consisting of a ball inside a ring which fell out if the machine was moved.

The first machine with a tilt mechanism was the "Multiple," made by the US manufacturer Henry Williams. The next step was an electric pivot whose tip came into contact with a metal ring if the machine was tilted, thereby creating an electrical circuit which ended the game.

The use of electricity may not have brought any radical changes to the pinball machine, but it did mean that light and sound could be added to make the machine more attractive. The year 1933 saw the first machine with electrically operated flippers, the "Contact," made by Henry Williams. The machines were battery operated until 1935, when new transformers allowed them to be operated from the mains. One new variation on the game was the kick-out-hole, where the ball was caught in a hole but could be dislodged by another ball. In Germany, a model was introduced with mechanical flaps which opened when they were hit by a ball: the maximum score on this machine was 130,000. This in turn developed into the lights-out game, where small lights could be turned out by hitting them with the ball.

Another major innovation came from Chicago, where Nick Nelson, an employee of Bally, invented the bumper: a spring-loaded cylinder which scores points when hit by the ball and bounces the ball off in another direction.

In Germany, the American bumper was known as the bomber, reflecting the increasingly warlike mood of Nazi Germany. Machines were covered in pro-war propaganda messages and the balls fell not into holes, but the mouths of cannons, which then fired them out again. These machines included the "Bombenfeuer," introduced in 1936.

But apart from electric flippers, the most important changes were in the visual appearance of the machines. Even the earliest bumpers bore lights which lit up when they were hit, and before long the whole playdeck was being illuminated. The first machines to show the score automatically on a display appeared in 1938: Bally's "Rocklite" was the first to have an illuminated scoreboard.

These displays gradually grew larger, and were painted with colorful designs on specific themes which the machines were named after. The display of the "Control Tower," for example, showed an aircraft which climbed as the score increased, but crashed in flames if the machine was tilted.

Pinball machines became increasingly popular in Europe, and particularly in Germany, but in their home country they came under increasing pressure. Coin-operated machines of all kinds had always been controversial and were often banned. Even the very first bagatelle games had holes marked "free ball" which delivered the ball back to the player for an extra game: the first pinball machine to give free games was the Rock-Ola "Flash" in 1935. This alone was enough to discredit pinball machines and put them in the category of illegal gaming machines. Bally's "Rocket" even paid out coins for specific scores; this led to vociferous protests and eventually to a ban on pinball machines in 1941.

The leading opponent of the machines was Fiorello La Guardia, the mayor of New York. La Guardia was an early master of the soundbite and photo opportunity, and personally smashed up a number of machines with a hammer. More than 11,000 pinball machines were destroyed in New York alone during this campaign.

In Europe, pinball continued to be regarded as a harmless form of entertainment. 1935 saw the introduction of machines which paid out free game tokens, but as they never paid out money they were not covered by gaming machine restrictions.

Pinball machines suffered another setback after the United States joined the Second World War: leading manufacturers were forced to start making machine guns, shells and parachutes.

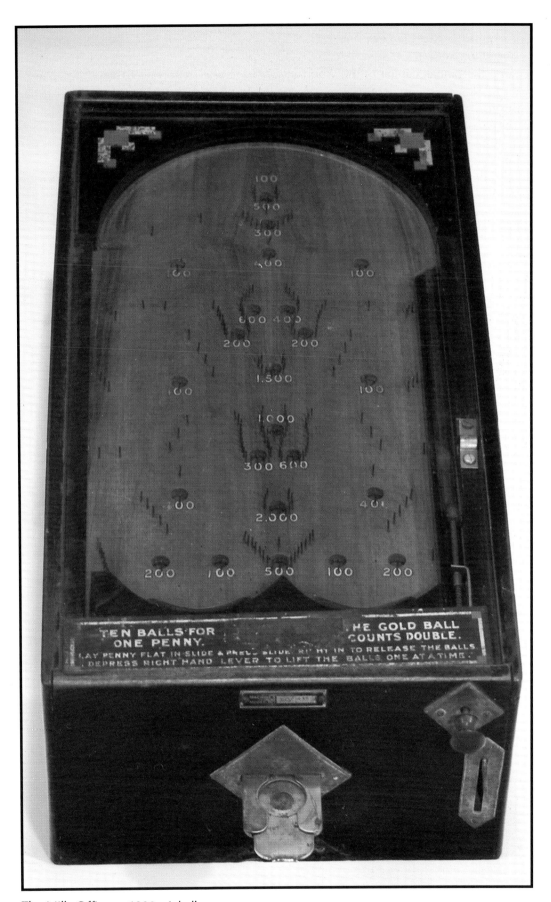

The Mills Office, a 1932 pinball game.

"Subway," a machine made by Genco in the 1930s

"Le Diamant," a French version of the American "Ballyhoo" (1931)

A variant of the German "Erbü Ball" from 1933

rbü Ball," one of
e first German
inball games,
ating from 1933

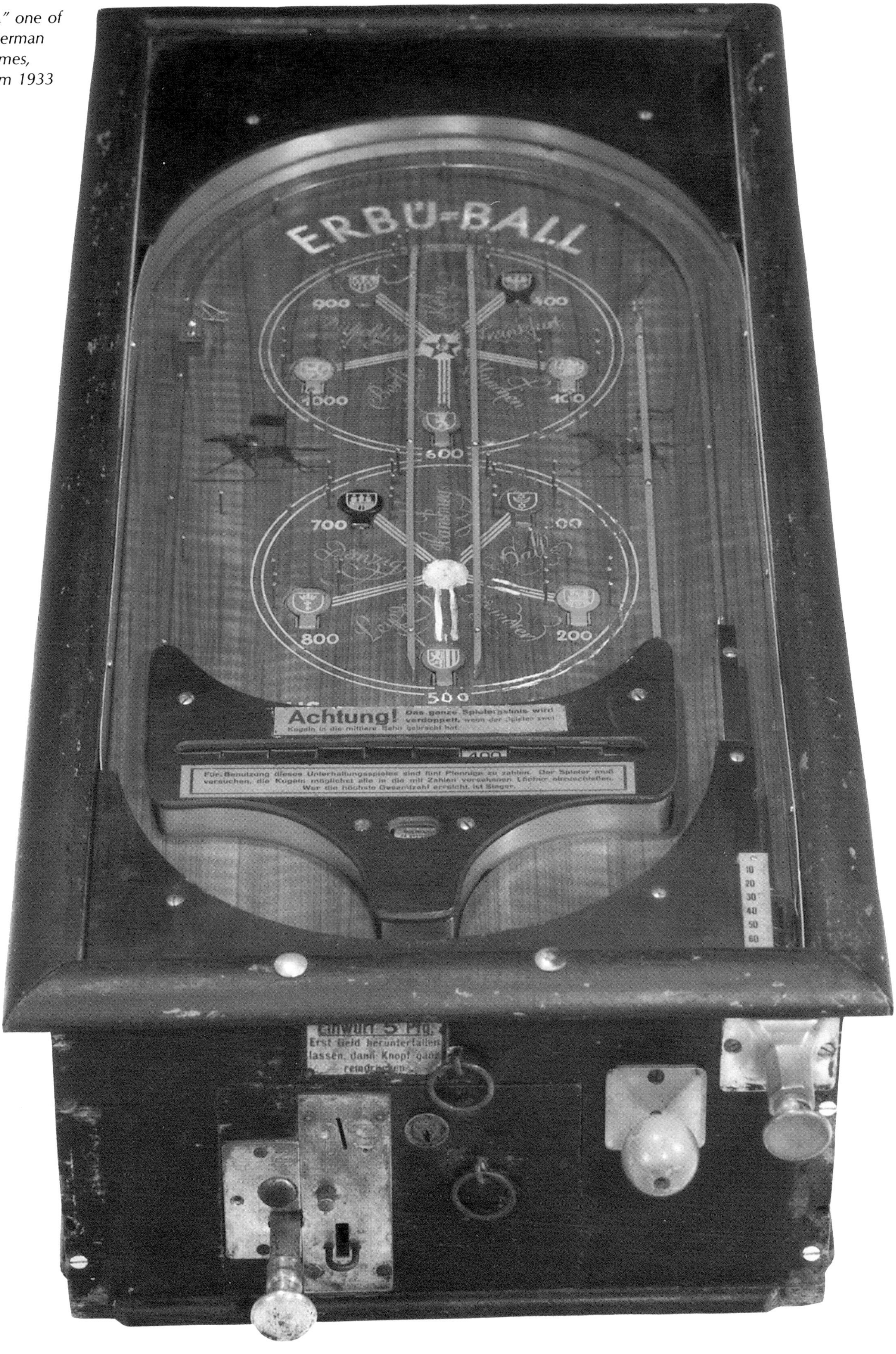

Ein farbenfrohes Kugelspiel

TURA BALL

Advertising brochure for "Tura Ball" (1933)

10 BÄLLE
5 PF.
20 BÄLLE
10 PF.

Überall polizeilich erlaubt!

C. M. SCHWARZ G. M. B. H.

Leipzig W 33 · Luppenstraße 1 · Fernruf 43090, 43093

Größtes Spezialunternehmen Europas · Vertreten in allen Hauptstädten Europas

Advertisement for the "Toby Ball" pinball machine, made by the Berlin company Heinrich Santelmann in 1932

Ein hochinteressantes Spiel,

ein großer Verdiener

in vielfarbiger Prachtausführung

Füße verstellbar und abschraubbar.

Farbige Prospekte, Preise und Aufstellerrabatte auf Anfrage zu Diensten.

HEINRICH SANTELMANN
Automatenfabrik
Berlin NW 21, Stromstr. 38 · Fernruf: Hansa 2056

STETS EINE BESONDERE NOTE HAT"

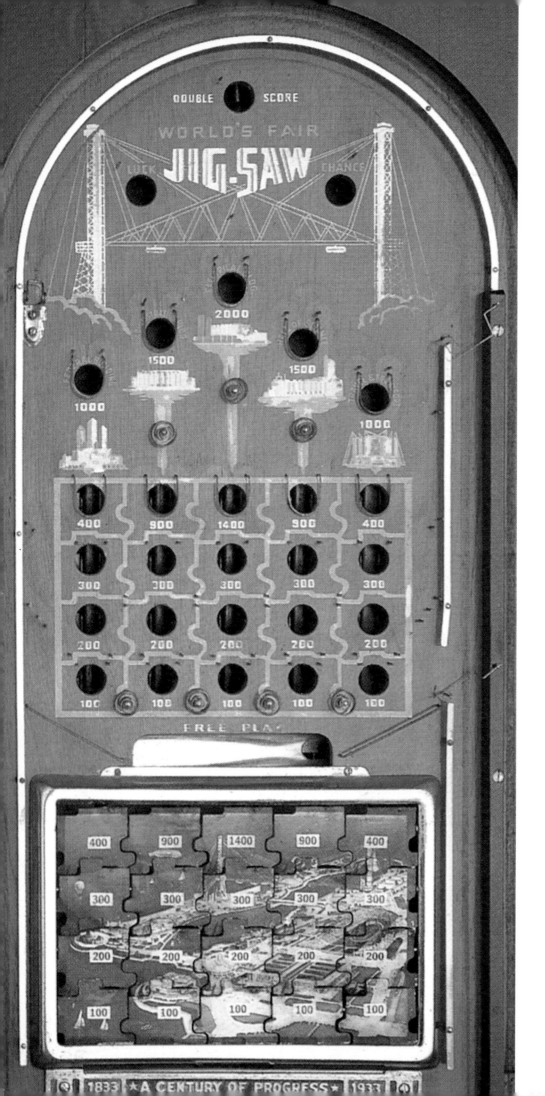

"World's Fair Jigsaw," a machine made by the Rock-Ola Manufacturing Corporation depicting the site of the 1933 World's Fair in San Francisco

"Tura Derby," made by the German company Tura Automatenfabrik in 1934

"Länderkampf" (International Match) made by Tränkner & Wietfeld in 1935

"Imo Weltflug" (Flying the World),
Jentzsch & Meerz, 1937

"Nürburgring," depicting Germany's famous motor racing circuit, was introduced at the 1939 Leipzig Spring Fair

Advertisement for "Imo Rennen" (Horse Racing), 1936

The "Turnier," one of Jentzsch & Meerz's most successful models (1935)

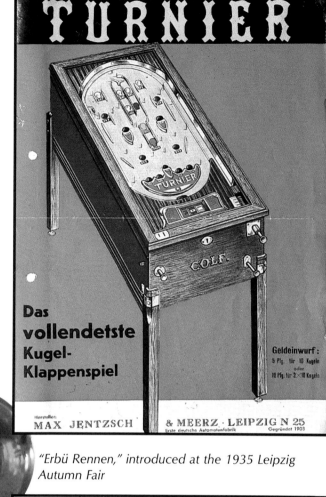

The "Imo Weltflug" was the first German machine with an illuminated display

"Erbü Rennen," introduced at the 1935 Leipzig Autumn Fair

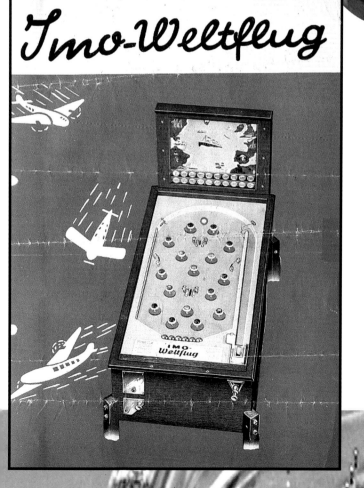

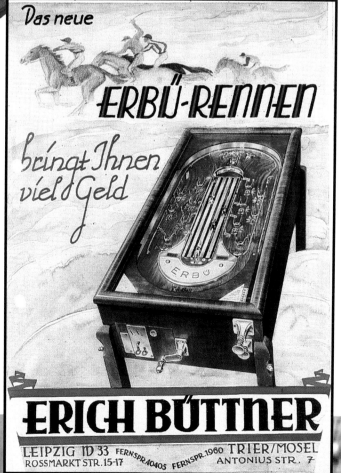

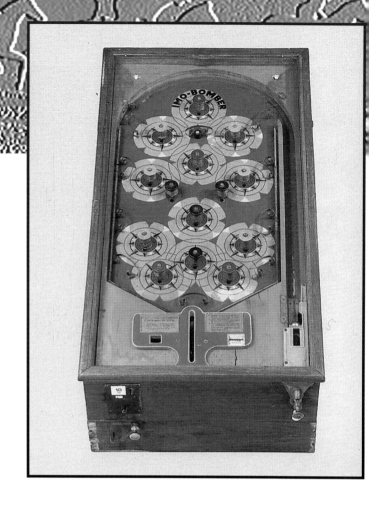

**Das Nadelspiel
in höchster Vollendung**

**ERBÜ-
BALL 1ᵇ**

ERICH BÜTTNER

Goldene Medaille Dresden 1932

TRIER a. MOSEL
ANTONIUSSTRASSE 7
FERNSPRECH-ANSCHLUSS 1960

LEIPZIG W 33
ROSSMARKTSTRASSE 15-17
FERNSPRECH-ANSCHLUSS 48405

Top left: *"Imo Rennen," a machine with a horse-racing theme made by Jentzsch & Meerz (1936)*
Above: *"Imo Bomber," an early example of a bumper machine (1937)*
Left: *"Erbü Ball," made by Erich Büttner in Leipzig*

"Favorit," a successful machine first used in 1939

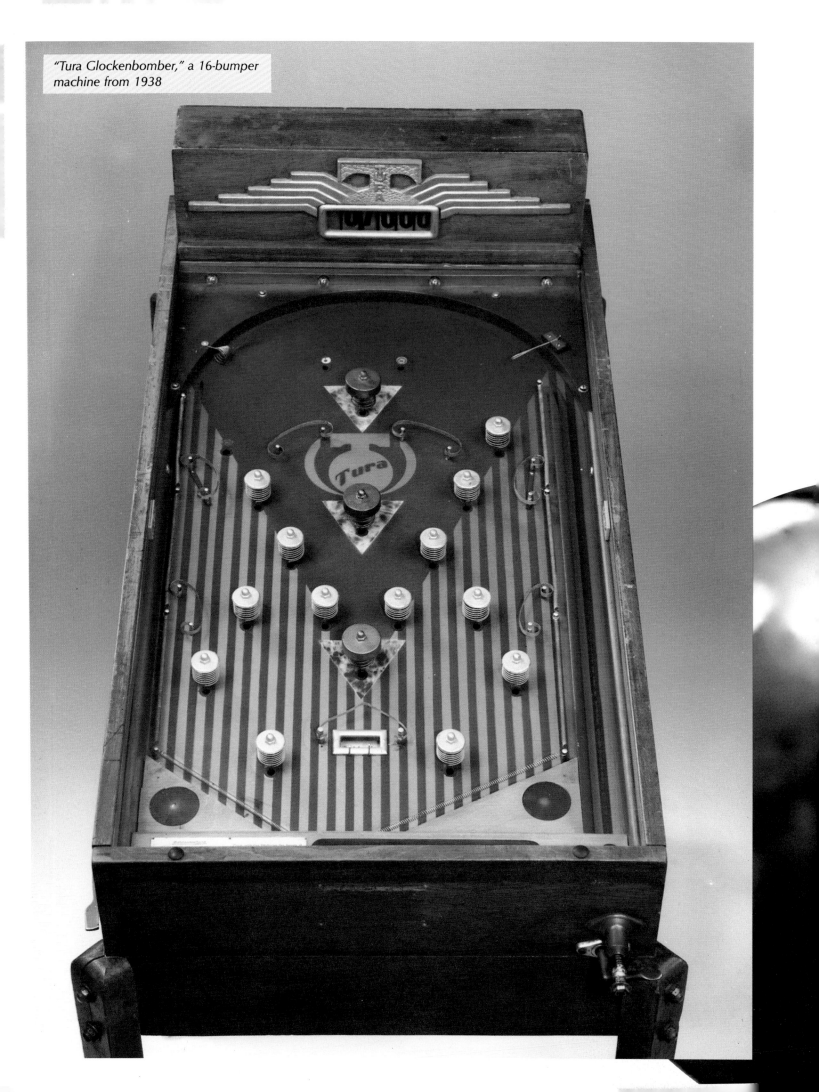

"Tura Glockenbomber," a 16-bumper machine from 1938

Left: "Bombenfeuer," a machine with a free ball facility made by Hannover-Automatengesellschaft in 1936
Below: "Brilliant Torero," manufactured by Bergmann & Co (1938)

Gottlieb's advertisement for the "Humpty Dumpty," the first machine with flippers (1947)

"Treff Gloria," made by Lignum GmbH (1953)

Right: the "Imo Spurt," made by Jentzsch & Meerz and dating from 1952, and (above) an advertisement for this machine

Above: Gottlieb's "Daisy May" (1954)

Right: "Shooting," a machine from the early 1950s

Bally "Beach Queens," 1958

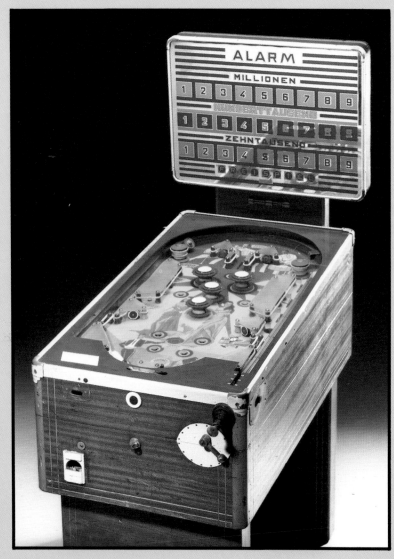

Above: "Alarm," made by Bergmann & Co (1956)

Below: Gottlieb "World Beauties" (1960)

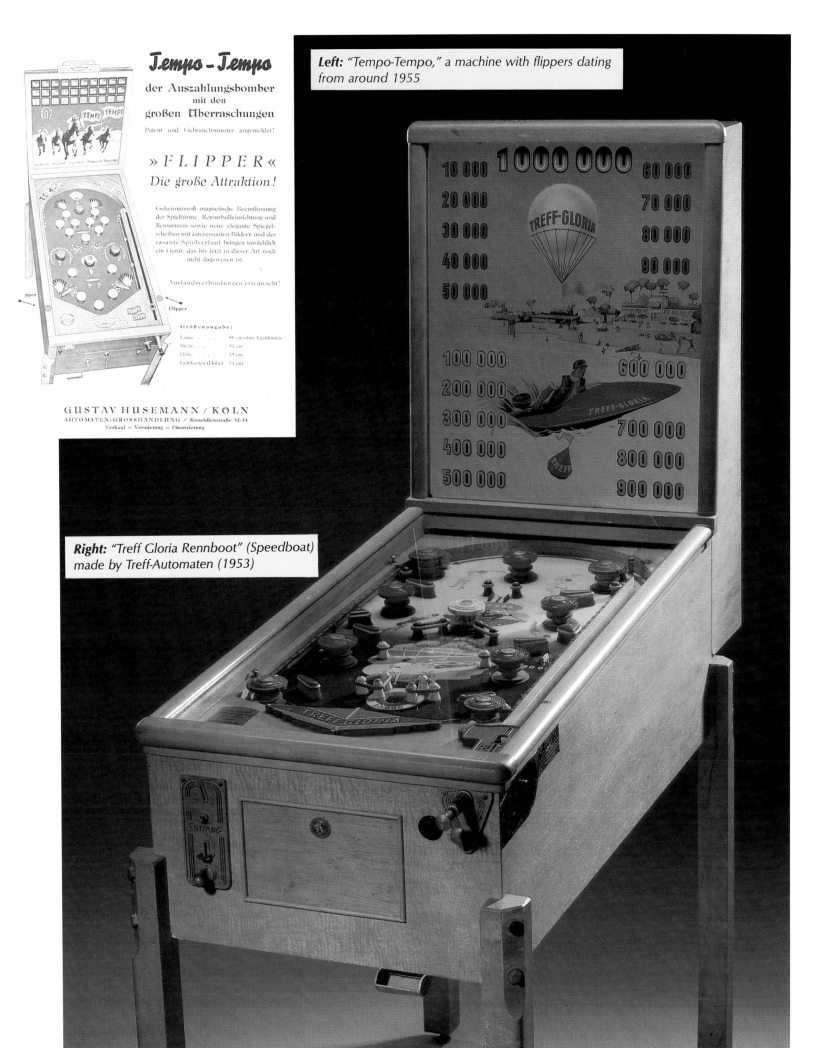

Tempo - Tempo

der Auszahlungsbomber
mit den
großen Überraschungen

Patent und Gebrauchsmuster angemeldet!

»FLIPPER«
Die große Attraktion!

Geheimnisvoll magnetische Beeinflussung
der Spieltürme, Retourballeinrichtung und
Retourturm sowie neue elegante Spiegel-
scheiben mit interessanten Bildern und der
rasante Spielverlauf bringen tatsächlich
ein Gerät, das bis jetzt in dieser Art noch
nicht dagewesen ist.

Auslandsverbindungen erwünscht!

Flipper

Größenangabe:

Länge . . . . . . 88 cm ohne Lichtkasten
Breite . . . . . . 54 cm
Höhe . . . . . . 35 cm
Lichtkasten (Höhe) 54 cm

GUSTAV HUSEMANN / KÖLN
AUTOMATEN-GROSSHANDLUNG / Komödienstraße 32-34
Verkauf – Vermietung – Finanzierung

Left: "Tempo-Tempo," a machine with flippers dating from around 1955

Right: "Treff Gloria Rennboot" (Speedboat) made by Treff-Automaten (1953)

THE GOLDEN AGE

Business was quiet in the pinball industry for several years after the Second World War, with manufacturers only gradually returning to production. The first successful machines of the post-war period were Gottlieb's "Stage Door Canteen" and Bally's "Victory Special." Most machines of this time had numbered bumpers which had to be hit in sequence or in specific combinations. 1946 saw the arrival of an important new manufacturer when Harry Williams founded Williams Manufacturing; his first machine was the "Suspense."

Another major step forward for pinball machines came in 1947 with the introduction of the flipper. Henry Mabs, of Gottlieb, designed a machine with a baseball theme in which, for the first time, the player was able to control two arms at the bottom end of the machine which stopped the ball from going out of play. The first "Humpty Dumpty" machine had three sets of flippers: at last the player could actively control the game. This innovation marked an abrupt end to the old-style pinball machines: the new generation of machines enjoyed immediate popularity and put the success of their predecessors in the shade.

The first European flipper machines followed shortly afterwards: the flippers were arranged differently on different machines, though they were usually located on the outer edge. They were less powerful than those of today, and it took several flips to get the ball up to the top of the machine. Later on, in the early 1950s, the number of flippers was reduced to a single pair.

The industry was dominated by Gottlieb and Williams, who began introducing increasingly lurid machines onto the market. Many of their designs were highly imaginative and greatly added to the visual appeal of the machine. The display of the Williams "Spark Plugs," for example, depicted racehorses which moved towards a finishing line as the score increased. One extremely popular machine was Gottlieb's "Knockout," which showed two boxers in action; another of the company's machines was the "Mermaid," with a fisherman whose net filled up as the number of points increased.

Until now, the score had been shown by a series of illuminated numbers marked in thousands, ten thousands and so on, and

the player had to add up the score themselves. For example a total of 1,240,000 points would have been shown as 1,000,000, 200,000 and 40,000. After 1950, machines used rotating dials marked with the numbers one to nine. In 1953, Williams brought out the "Gun Club" and "Struggle Bunnies," which had seven score reels and showed scores up to 9,999,999.

At the same time, a number of manufacturers were trying to redesign the game itself. In the 1958 "Turf Champ," the player chose one of six horses by pressing a button before starting the game. All six horses moved as the score increased, and if the player's selection was first past the post, they were given a free game.

One very well-known machine was the "Queen of Hearts." Based on playing cards, this machine used different paths and card combinations to win free games. The "Hot Diggity" (1956) gave free games if the player achieved specific combinations of letters by hitting targets. Williams built a bumper which sank below the playing surface in certain situations, allowing the ball to reach bonus areas. This game proved very popular, but was also very expensive to produce and was soon withdrawn from the market. Only two models continued to be built in small numbers.

The next major advance after the invention of flippers was the introduction of the multi-player game. Gottlieb's "Super Jumbo" (1954) was the first to allow four people to play at the same time, giving an exciting new element of competition by achieving the highest score. Gottlieb's slogan was "It's more fun to compete." However, because the "Super Jumbo" had to show four players' scores, there was only room for three-digit scores, and this problem was not solved until the 1970s.

In March 1955 Williams followed suit with the four-player game "Race the Clock." The third giant of the industry, Bally, produced only one machine during the 1950s, "Balls-a-Poppin," a two-player game with up to seven balls per game.

The 1950s were the golden years of the pinball machine, and their popularity was not dented by the passing of very strict

gambling laws in the United States in 1951. Pinball machines which paid out money were immediately banned, and this ban was soon extended to other machines, such as those giving large numbers of free games: some gave up to 999, and owners often paid rewards.

But pinball remained a popular leisure activity. In the words of one of Gottlieb's advertisements: "Amusement Pinball – as American as baseball and hot dogs!"

"Wild Card," a Williams machine
with a playing-card
theme (1977)

Above: "Darts," with an unusual design by Williams (1960)

Left: Advertisement for the new Williams four-player
"Big Chief" (1965)

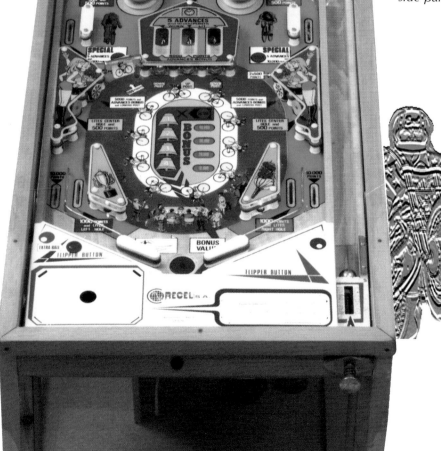

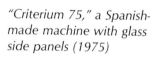

"Criterium 75," a Spanish-made machine with glass side panels (1975)

"Jack in the Box": a four-player version of Gottlieb's "Jumping Jack"

Gottlieb "Hi-Score Pool" (1967)

Williams "Jubilee" (1973)

Bally "Lady Luck" (1968)

Gottlieb "Surf Champ" (1976)

A Bally machine featuring the daredevil motorcyclist,
Evel Knievel (1977)

Bally "Ro Go," with a Norseman motif

Bally "Captain Fantastic," featuring Elton John (1976)

Bally "Harvest" with a typical early '60s display (1964)

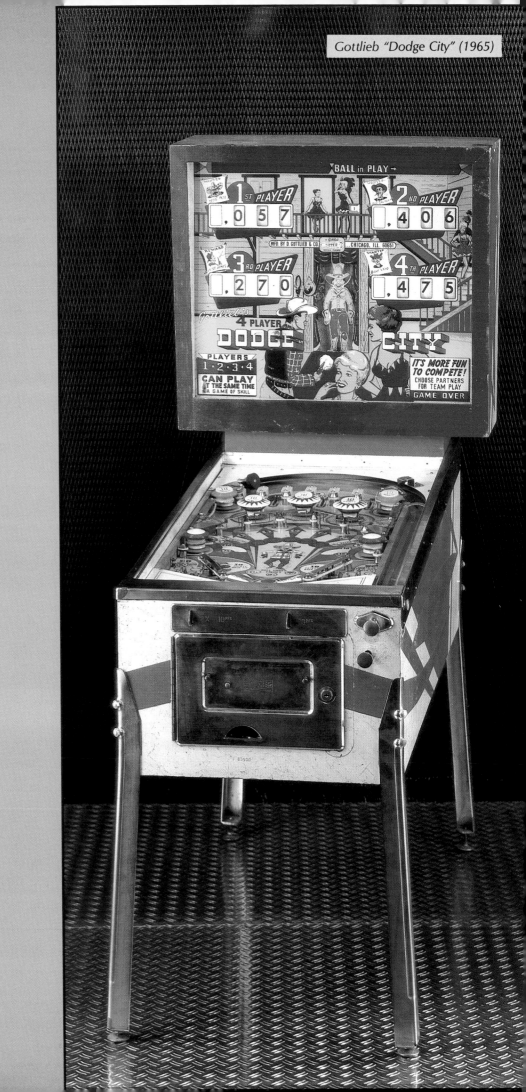

EUROMAT

Hunderttausend

Millionen

"Euromat," an unusual machine made by Aisch & Melchers (1960)

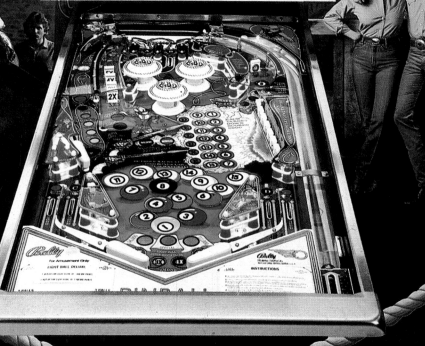

Wenn Sie Erfolg suchen, werden Sie beim Hot Doggin' fündig!

Große Spielfläche ermöglicht große Bounuswertungen

Das Vervollständigen von S–K–I, F–U–N und H–O–T–D–O–G–G–I–N beleuchtet beim 1. Mal 30.000 Bonus und Freikugelmöglichkeit am Kugelauswurfloch, beim 2. Mal erhält der Spieler eine Freikugel und für jedes weitere Beleuchten ein Freispiel. Der Bonusmultiplikator wird durch das Treffen der Fallziele der Reihenfallzieleinheit erhöht.

Das Treffen des Kugelauswurfloches wird auf 4fache Weise belohnt

Jedes Treffen des Kugelauswurfloches zählt 500 Punkte. Diese Wertung wird bei entsprechender Beleuchtung auf Freikugel, Freispiel oder 25.000 Punkte erhöht.

3 Fallzieleinheiten fordern zu gezielten Schüssen heraus

Leuchtende, farbfrohe Zeichnungen prägen sich jedem Spieler sofort ein

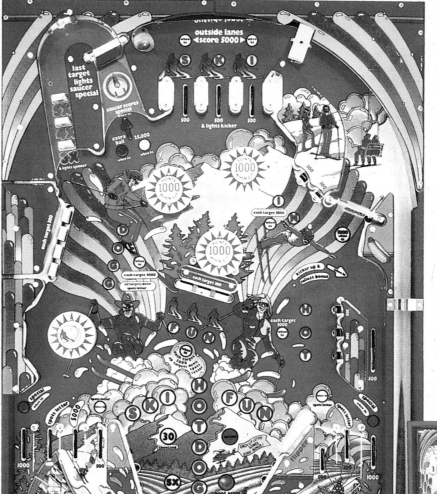

Special Kickereinheit sorgt für zusätzlichen Kugellauf

Die rechte Kickerbahn wird beleuchtet und der Kicker aufgerichtet, wenn die Kugel durch die obere „K"-Bahn gerollt ist. Rollt die Kugel bei aufgerichtetem Kicker in die Kickerbahn, wird der erzielte Bonus zum Ergebnis hinzuaddiert und die Kugel wieder ausgekickt.

S–K–I beleuchtet 5.000 Punkte

Das Vervollständigen von S–K–I beleuchtet an den oberen Kugelbahnen 5.000 Punkte. Die S–K–I Kugelbahnen beleuchten außerdem die darunterliegenden Schlagtürme für 1.000 Punkte.

Bally

PINBALL DIVISION

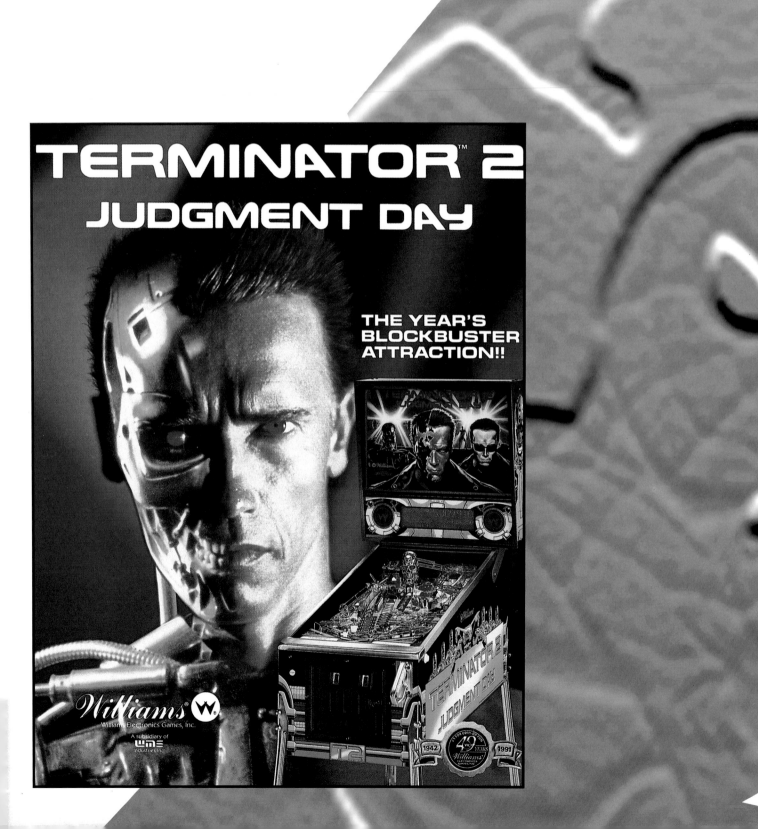

Gottlieb "Spiderman" (1979)

PINBALL FEVER AND THE ROCK ERA

Pinball machines had competition. At the beginning of the 1960s, other slot machines were gaining an increasing share of the lucrative entertainment market, and pinball experienced a distinct decline in Europe after flourishing during the previous decade. Only Gottlieb and Williams continued turning out new and innovative machines in their efforts to retain the loyalty of players.

One idea from the early 1960s was the add-a-ball system. Instead of giving free plays, the 1960 "Flipper" extended the game by providing extra balls. This variation on the game proved highly successful, not least because it was a clever way of getting round problems with the law. In the United States at least, free plays were suspected of being disguised rewards for gambling, and the add-a-ball system solved this problem. The "Flipper" was so popular that Gottlieb produced a whole series of related machines: the "Flipper Parade" and "Flipper Fair" (both 1961), followed by the "Flipper Clown" and "Flipper Cowboy" (both 1962).

Another new feature was drop targets. The playdeck of the "Vagabond," introduced by Williams in 1962, had a small target at its center which sank below the playdeck when hit by the ball. A later development of this feature was spinning targets: small targets suspended by a fine wire which spun at high speed if hit, with each rotation adding to the score.

These innovations helped the pinball industry to improve its sales somewhat during the mid-'60s and to regain popularity. Leading manufacturers began production again: the most important of these was Bally, which had stopped building pinball machines in 1953. The company's "Moon Shot" proved a dramatic success.

But the main differences between pinball machines were still their displays. Space travel was a recurring theme; so were playing-cards and pool. Despite the wide variety of subject matter, the styles were very similar, which was not particularly surprising: all the displays for Bally, Gottlieb and Williams machines were designed by a single agency, Advertising Posters of Chicago.

In the early 1970s changing tastes were reflected in an increasing number of designs featuring prehistoric or mythical motifs. One particularly successful design was Bally's "Fireball" (1972), whose display featured a red monster hurling fireballs at the player. This design was repeated on the playdeck, and Bally sold 3815 of these machines.

Although pinball machines had reached a new stage of technical advancement, Bally introduced a new refinement in 1969 with their "Bazaar" machine, which included zipper flippers. Two flippers on the bottom edge of the playdeck closed if the ball hit specific targets, stopping it from passing through. This meant that the ball could be shot off towards the top again, or caught, held and then aimed off in a particular direction. This variation was so popular that Bally immediately brought out another model, the "Capersville." This proved the most successful of all Bally machines: the company sold 5120.

Other manufacturers imitated this idea and began experimenting with different types of flipper. In the Williams "Hayburner II," the length of the flippers was increased from 2 to 3 inches to achieve greater power, and from now on short flippers were only used as additions around the edge of the playdeck. The longest flippers of any machine were those of the 1970 "Big Flipper," at five inches.

Another attempt to make pinball machines more popular was made by changing the rules of the game. In 1971, Gottlieb produced the "Challenger," designed solely for two-person play. It had no display: instead the two players stood at either end and tried to shoot the ball into their opponent's goal. Challenger was not particularly successful, perhaps because it lost sight of the idea of pitting humans against machines. Only around 500 of these machines were sold.

Another new machine from Williams introduced a time factor into the game. Its "Travel Time" (1973) gave the player sixty time credits which gradually ran out. Skillful ball handling could be used to stop the clock and make the game longer.

At the height of the hippy and flower power era of the late '60s, pinball machines achieved unprecedented popularity: this was probably their finest hour. In 1975, they became the star of their own rock musical movie which highlighted the strong links between pinball and rock music. Tommy featured The Who and was produced by their lead singer Roger Daltrey. Its title song, Pinball Wizard, became a top ten hit around the world. Inevitably, a pinball machine called the "Wizard" appeared in the same year, with a display depicting Roger Daltrey and his co-star. Bally sold 10,005 "Wizard" machines.

Another film about pinball was Tilt (1978), starring Brooke Shields as a player who earns a good living from competitive pinball. The high point of the film is a duel between her and another champion player. Tilt was not only a financial flop, but also attracted criticism for depicting pinball as a form of gambling.

Another rock-based design which sold in record numbers was Bally's "Captain Fantastic" (1976), which depicted Elton John surrounded by keyboards and guitars; 16,155 of these machines were sold.

But as the general enthusiasm for pinball reached its zenith, a new and major rival was beginning to appear. The first video games had arrived.

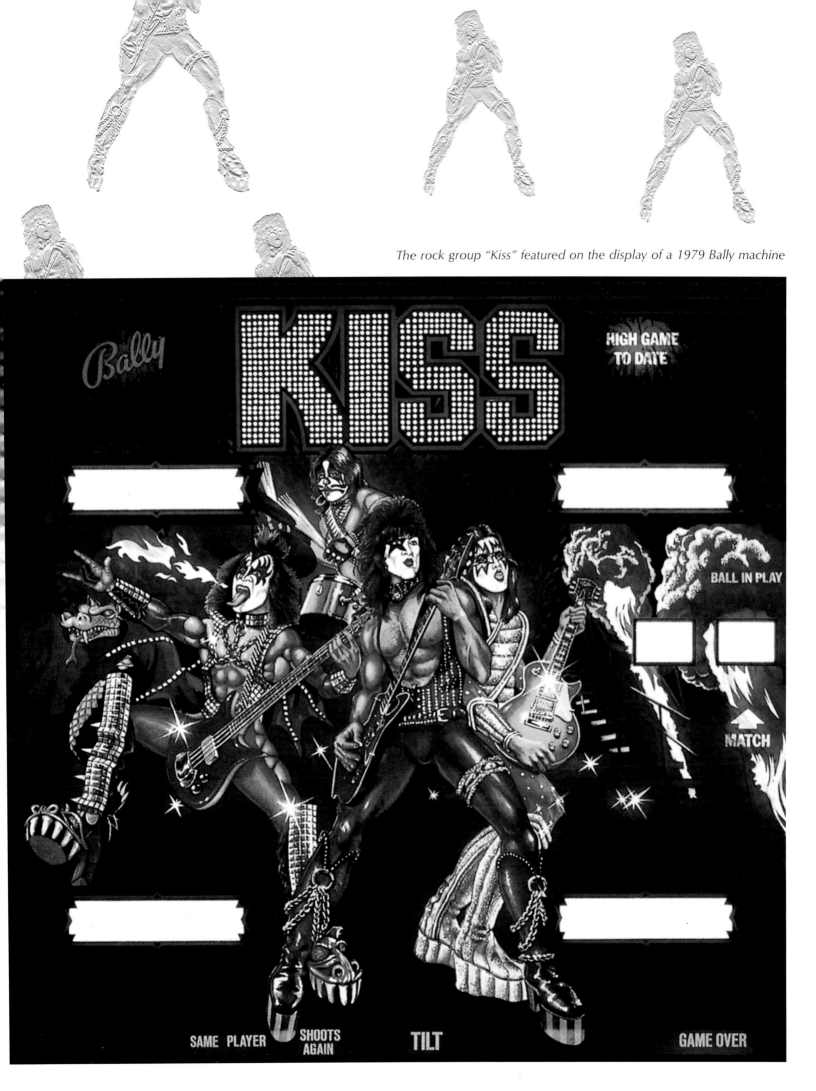

The rock group "Kiss" featured on the display of a 1979 Bally machine

Meine Damen und Herren ...
DIE ROLLING STONES

Bally

KISS
macht die Musik

Kassen zum Küssen

Bally AT9 1

Gottlieb's GENIE

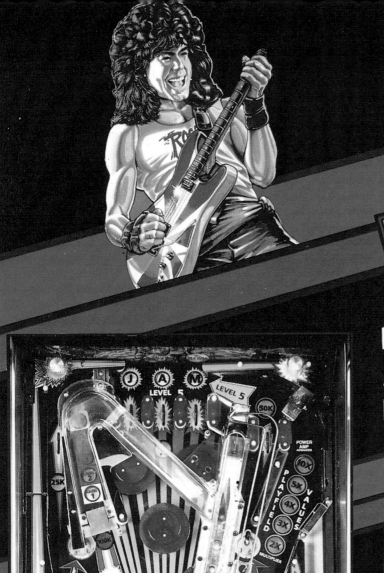

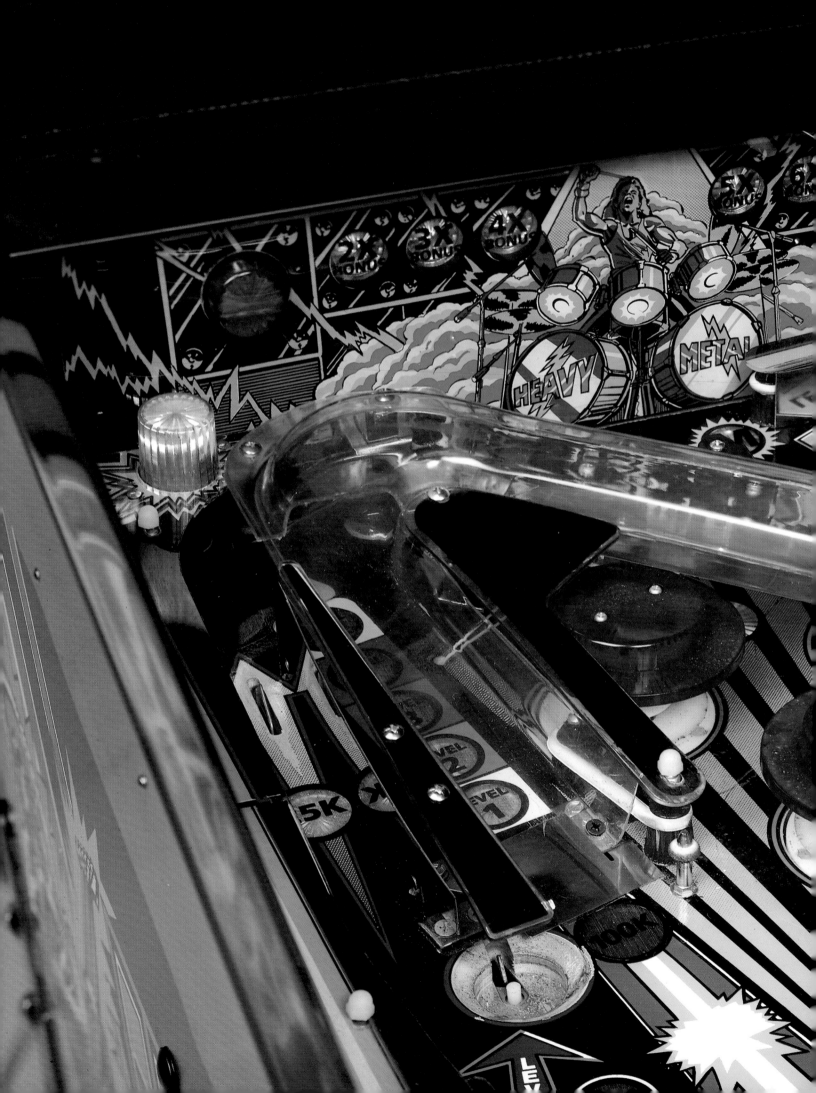

THE RISE OF THE MICROCHIP

• •

The first video game, introduced in 1973, was a very simple affair: a Ping-Pong game which involved hitting an imaginary ball back and forth with two equally imaginary bats. No-one really took it very seriously, but this was the vanguard of a new form of technology which threatened to make the pinball machine obsolete.

Meanwhile, though, micro-electronics was being used to improve the technology of the pinball machine. The first machine to be operated by a microchip rather than a system of relays and wires was Micro Games' "Spirit of 76." This machine replaced the traditional scoreboard with a digital display, but its playdeck was so unattractively designed that only around 100 were ever made. But the new digital display attracted great interest, as the major obstacle to improving traditional electric machines had been the scoring system. In a fast-moving game, with one or more balls hitting a number of targets in quick succession, the revolving dials simply could not keep up and many of the points scored never registered on the scoreboard. But digital scoring uses an electronic memory to store every score, even when the ball is moving at high speed. This also meant that more and more targets could be fitted and the game became much faster.

In the spring of 1976, Allied Leisure Industries brought out the first successful electronic pinball machine, the "Dyn-O-Mite." The market leader, Bally, followed suit with the "Eight Ball" in 1977. Its electronic memory not only recorded all the rapid succession of hits, but remembered all the scores that a player had achieved and carried them forward into the next game. Bally produced 20,230 of these successful machines.

Another advance came in the form of the Williams "Gorgar," the world's first talking pinball machine. A red monster constantly roars: "Me Gorgar, beat me," and when the score reaches certain points it groans: "You hurt Gorgar."

Despite these novelties, manufacturers could not stave off the decline of the pinball machine. Video games had long since moved on from the first primitive Ping-Pong games, and attracted players with ever more sophisticated computer animation. Young people drifted away from the traditional pinball machine and only the most high-tech of multi-level pinball games were able to compete with the lure of the video game. Many manufacturers moved out of the market altogether or were taken over by leading companies in the entertainment industry. Some traditional companies survived because a small minority of pinball fans continued to buy reproductions of traditional machines. In 1984, when Gottlieb's new owner, Columbia Pictures, decided to shut down production and there were rumors that Williams was in serious financial difficulties, the era of the pinball machine seemed to be over.

DER
FLIPPER,
DER
ABRÄUMT

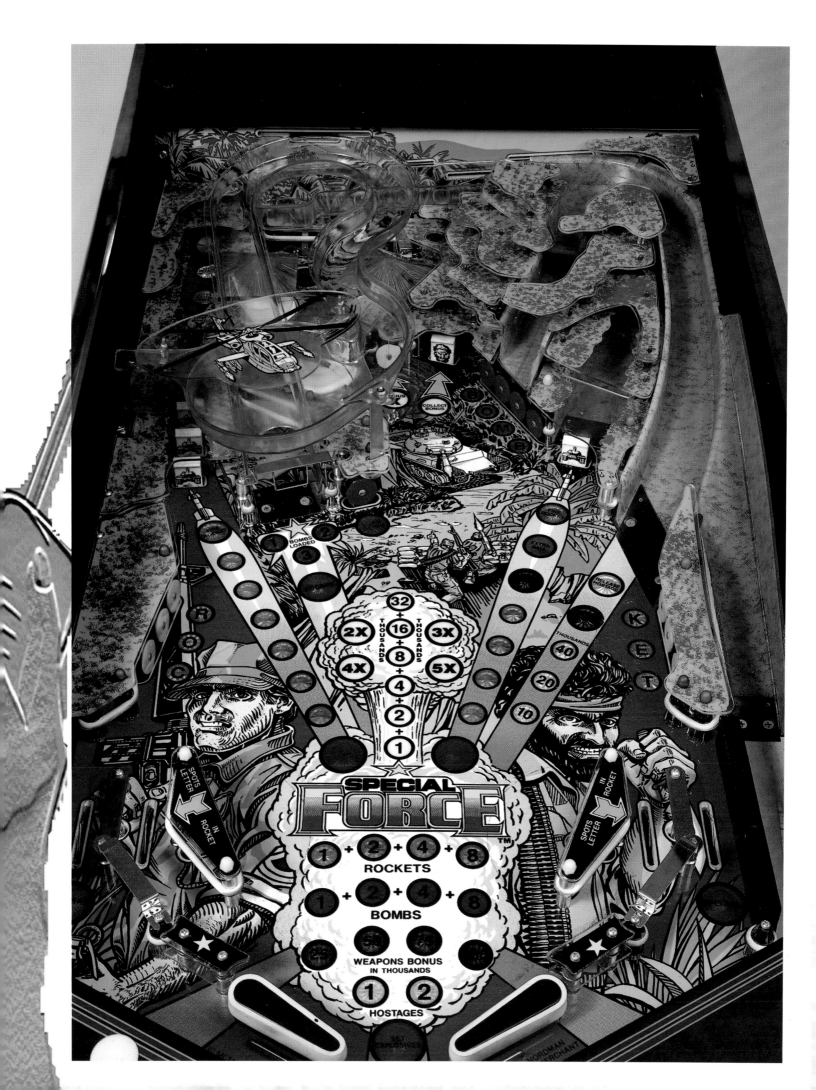

ALL IS NOT LOST

· · · · · · · · · · · · · · · · · · ·

But there was still life left in
the pinball machine. Many
manufacturers, including companies
which had previously made only
video games, realized there was still
plenty of potential in the market. In
Germany, for example, sales
increased by 50 per cent in 1985
and by 100 per cent in 1986, with
63,200 machines installed in bars,
restaurants and amusement arcades.
Since the mid-1980s, pinball has
regained its status as a popular form
of leisure entertainment. It owes its
continued success to the same basic
ideas as the very first machines: the
fascination of flashing lights and
high-speed action. Pinball still tests
our skills and reactions to the limit.
It still gives us the simple pleasure of
beating a piece of machinery, and of
snatching a last-minute victory from
the jaws of defeat.

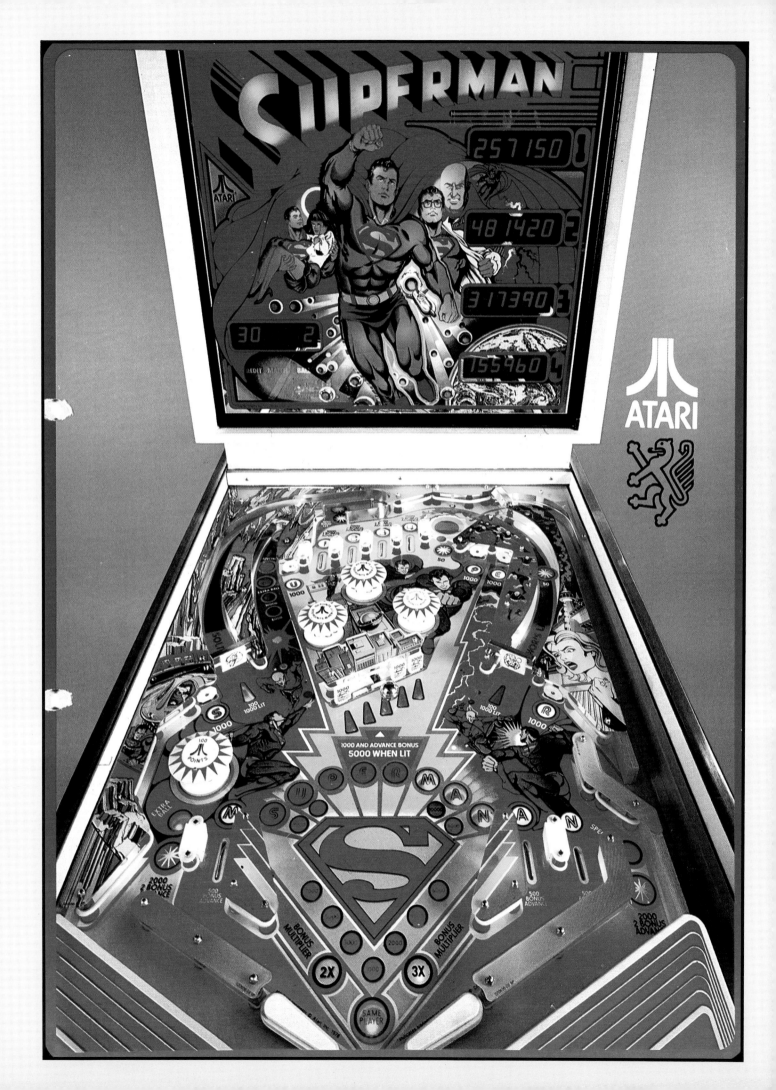

The display on Bally's "Haunted House" –
a multi-level game

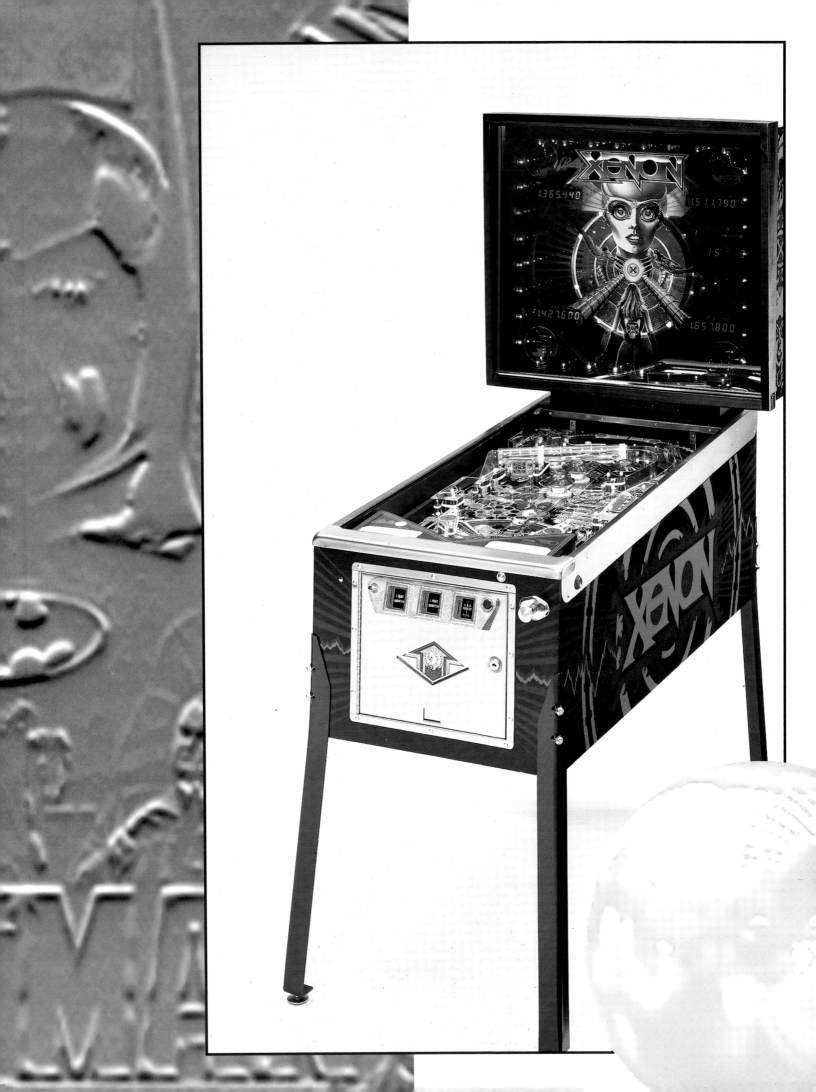

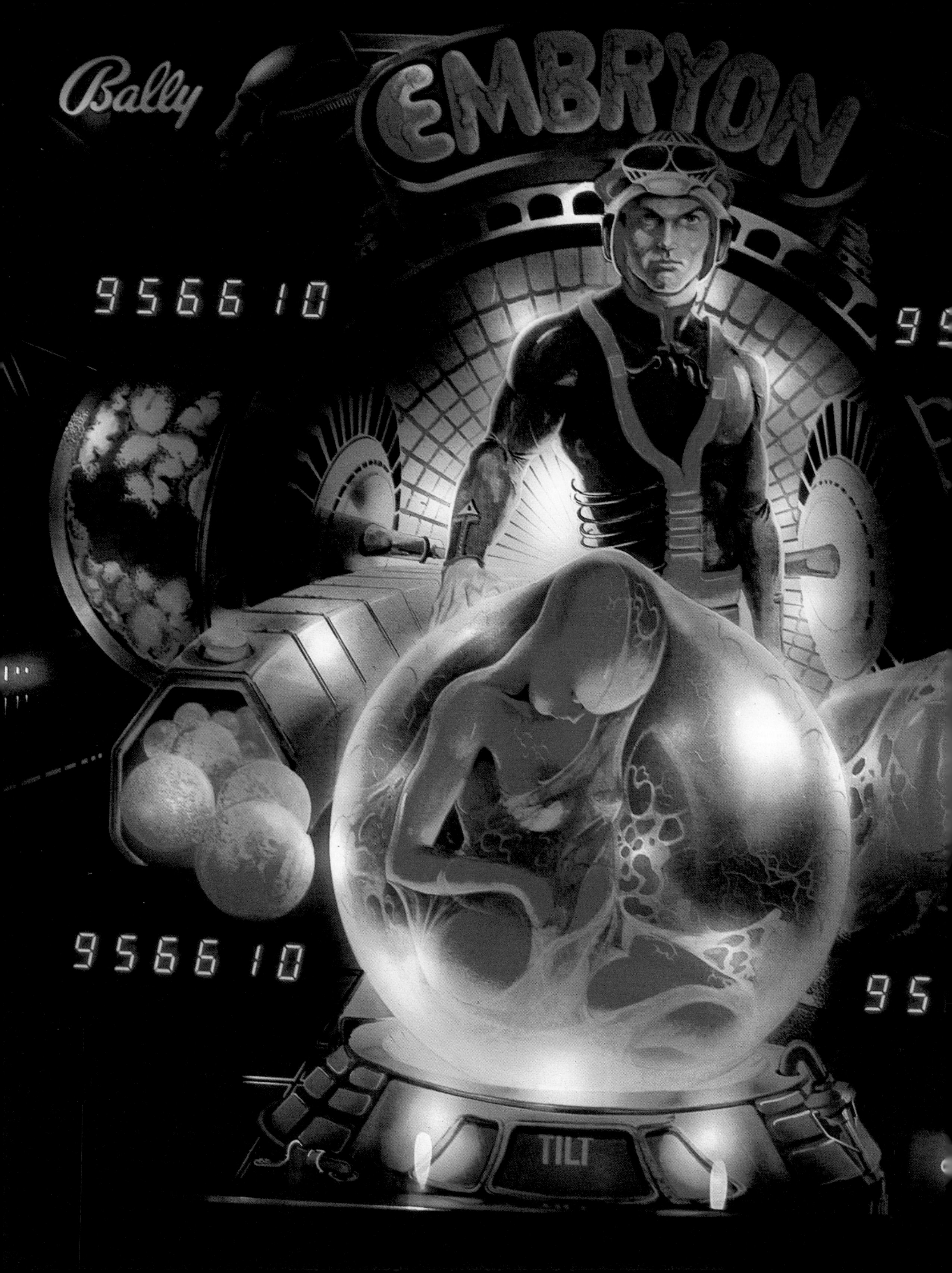
Bally
EMBRYON
956610
956610
TILT

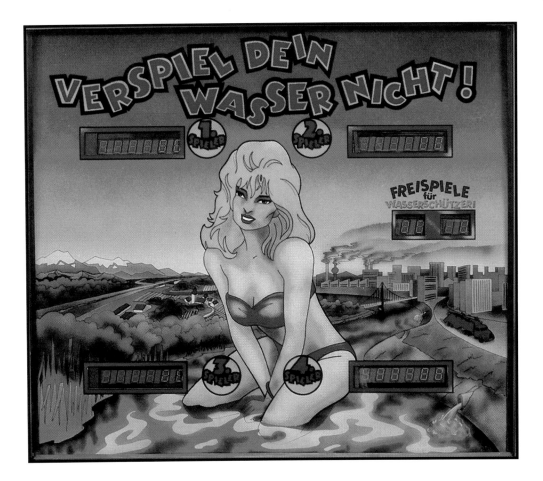

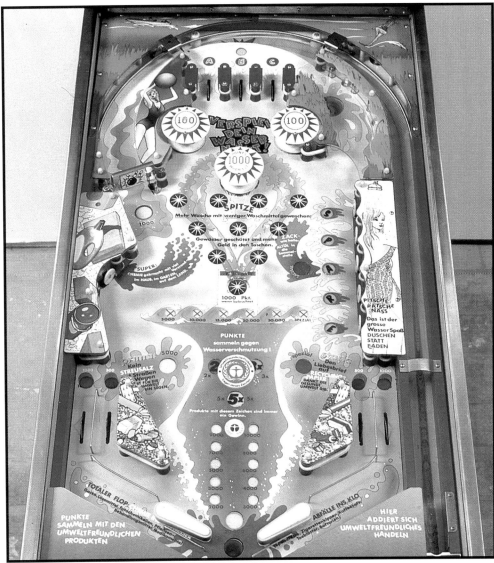

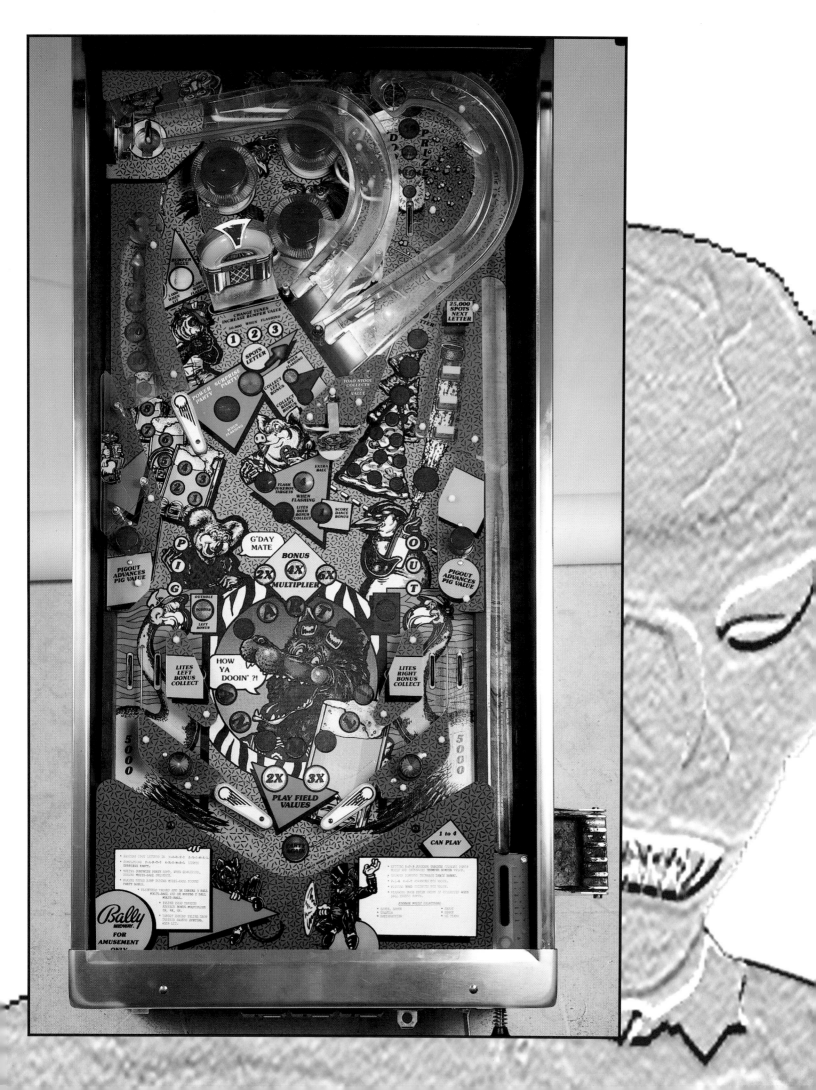

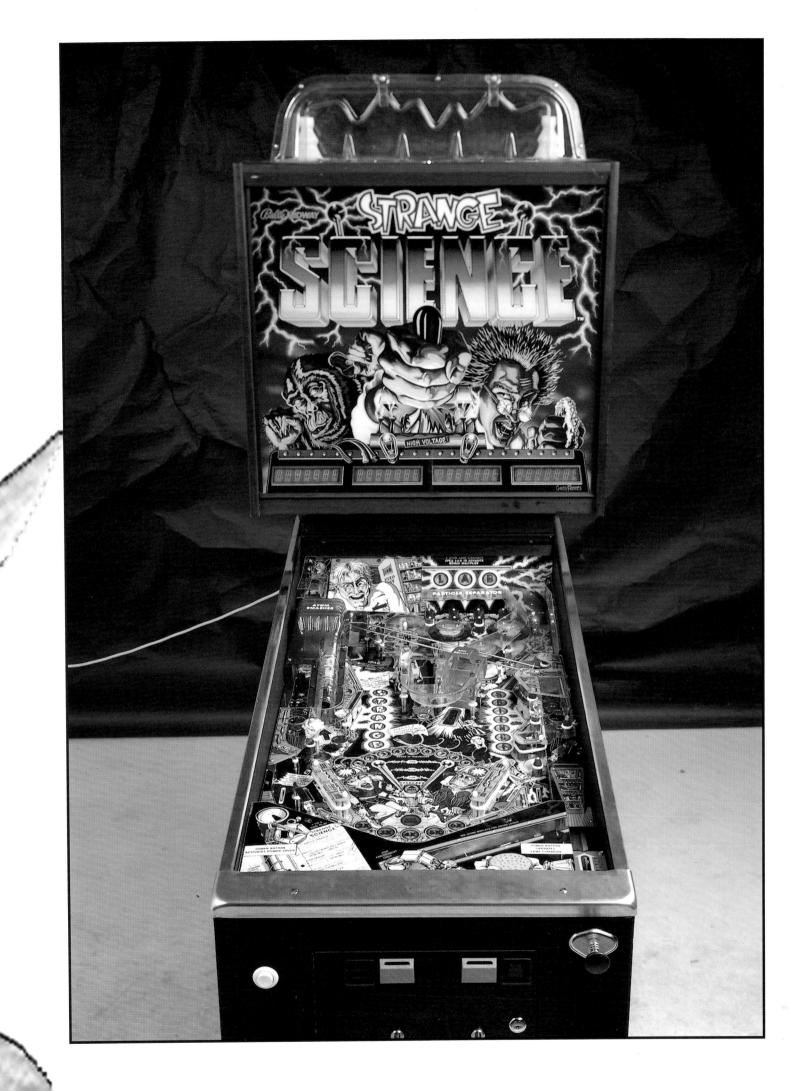

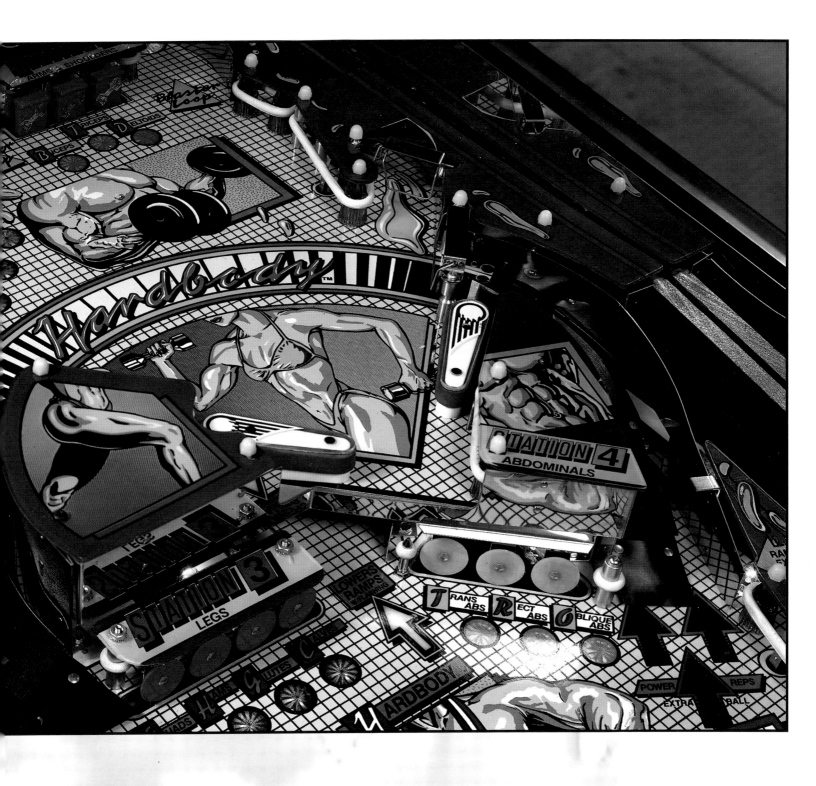

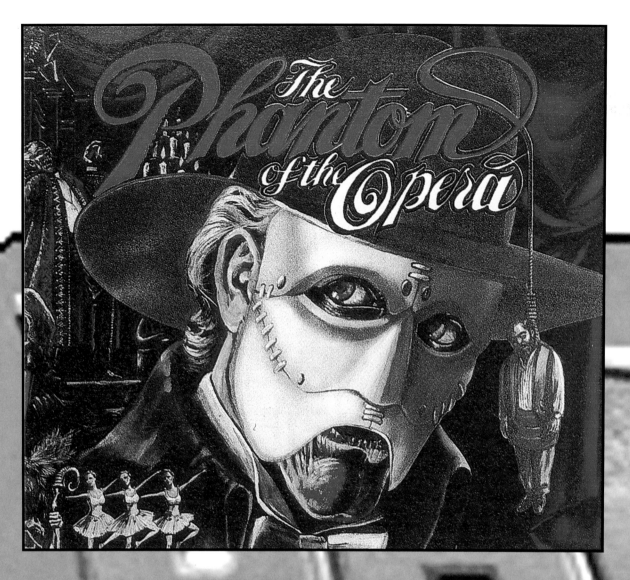

BACK TO THE FUTURE
THE PINBALL

BACKBOX NOW WITH **QUICK-LOC™** LOCKING SYSTEM

FEATURING THE HIT MUSIC **DOUBLEBACK** FROM ZZ TOP & **BACK IN TIME** AND **POWER OF LOVE** BY HUEY LEWIS AND THE NEWS

Featuring Quality Coin Doors and Validators from **COIN CONTROLS**